THE MOST REQUESTED
Songs of the '90s

Cherry Lane Music Company
Director of Publications/Project Editor: Mark Phillips

ISBN 978-1-4768-8960-3

T0057472

CONTENTS

Achy Breaky Heart
(Don't Tell My Heart)

Words and Music by
Don Von Tress

tell my fin - ger - tips they won't be reach - ing out for you no
watch out for my mind. It might be walk - ing out on me to -

more. ____
day. ____ But { Don't tell my heart, } my
{ don't tell my heart, }
{ Don't tell my heart, }

ach - y break - y heart. ____ I just don't think he'd un - der -

stand. And if you tell my heart, my ach - y break - y heart, ___ he

6

might blow _ up and kill this man.   Ooh. _____

man.

Don't tell my heart, my ach-y break-y heart. I just don't think he'd un-der-

stand. And if you tell my heart, my ach-y break-y heart, he

might blow up and kill this man. Ooh.

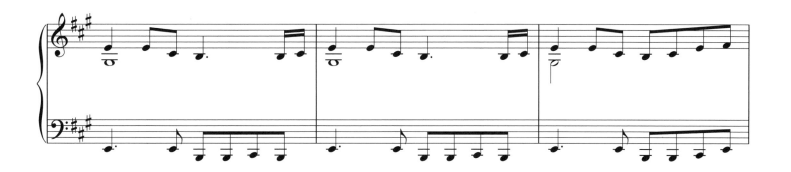

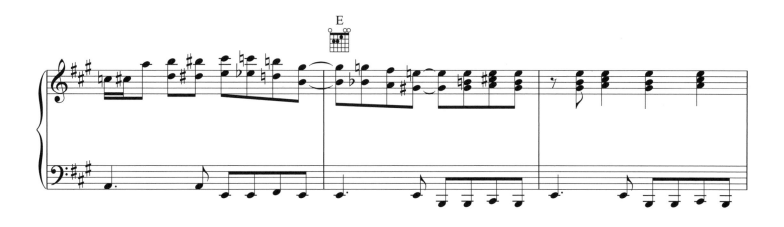

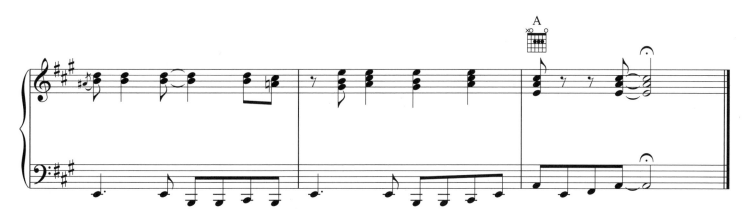

All I Wanna Do

Words and Music by
Kevin Gilbert, David Baerwald,
Sheryl Crow, Wyn Cooper
and Bill Bottrell

back to the phone com-pa-ny, the rec-ord store, too. Well, they're _ noth-ing like

Chorus

Bil-ly and me. _ 'Cause all I wan-na do is have some fun, _____ I got a feel-

-ing I'm not the on - ly one. All I wan-na do is have some fun,

_____ I got a feel - ing I'm not the on - ly one. All I wan-na

do   is have some   fun, ____   un - til   the   sun comes   up   o - ver

San - ta Mon - i - ca Bou - le - vard. ____

San - ta Mon - i - ca Bou - le - vard. __

Oth-er - wise ___ the bar ___ is ours, and the day and the night and the

car wash, too. ___ The match - es and the Buds and the

clean ___ and dirt - y cars, the sun and the moon. But all I wan - na

D.S. al Coda

Additional Lyrics

3. I like a good beer buzz early in the morning,
   And Billy likes to peel the labels from his bottles of Bud
   And shred them on the bar.
   Then he lights every match in an oversized pack,
   Letting each one burn down to his thick fingers
   Before blowing and cursing them out.
   And he's watching the Buds as they spin on the floor.
   A happy couple enters the bar dancing dangerously close to one another.
   The bartender looks up from his want ads.
   Chorus

Are You Gonna Go My Way

Words by Lenny Kravitz

Music by
Lenny Kravitz and Craig Ross

done.
one.

So that's why
So tell me why

you've got to try,
we've got to die

you've got to breathe and have some fun.
and kill each oth-er one by one.

Though I'm not paid,
We've got to love

I play this game,
and rub-a-dub,

and I won't stop un-til I'm done.
we've got to dance and be in love.

But what I real-ly

want to know___ is:_____ Are you gon-na go my

way? And I got to, got to know._

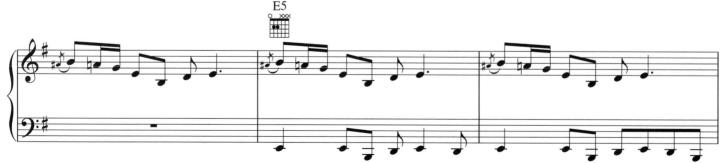

to know. _____

Play 4 times

E D   A D A

E D   A D A   Play 7 times

E D   N.C.

Are you gon-na go my way?

'Cause ba-by, I

got to know. __

...Baby One More Time

Words and Music by
Max Martin

Oh, ba-by, ba-by. Oh, ba-by, ba-by.

Oh, ba-by, ba-by, how was I sup-posed __ to know __ that
Oh, ba-by, ba-by, the rea-son I breathe __ is you. __

some-thing was-n't right here? Oh, ba-by, ba-by, I should-n't have let __ you go. __
Boy, you've got me blind - ed. Oh, pret-ty ba-by, there's noth-ing that I __ would-n't

N.C.

Oh, ba - by, ba - by.   Oh, ba - by, ba - by.

Cm   G7/B   E♭   Fm Gsus G

Oh, ba - by, ba - by, how was I sup - posed __ to know? __

A♭maj7   B♭   Fm7   A♭ B♭

Oh, pret - ty ba - by, I should - n't have let __ you go. _____ I must con - fess __

Cm   G7/B G7   E♭   Fm Gsus G

__ that my lone - li - ness __ is kill - ing me now. _____ Don't you know I still be - lieve __

Barely Breathing

Words and Music by
Duncan Sheik

Believe

Words and Music by
Brian Higgins, Stuart McLennen,
Paul Barry, Stephen Torch,
Matt Gray and Tim Powell

*Recorded a half step higher.
**Vocal written one octave higher than sung.

taacerax

Believe

Words and Music by
Brian Higgins, Stuart McLennen,
Paul Barry, Stephen Torch,
Matt Gray and Tim Powell

Moderate Disco beat

No mat-ter how_ / What am I sup-

hard I try___ / posed to do,___ you keep push-ing me a-side_ and I can't_ / sit a-round and wait for you,_ and I can't_

*Recorded a half step higher.
**Vocal written one octave higher than sung.

Copyright © 1998 PB SONGS LTD., XENOMANIA MUSIC and 119 SONGS
All Rights for PB SONGS LTD. Controlled and Administered by UNIVERSAL - POLYGRAM INTERNATIONAL PUBLISHING INC.
All Rights for XENOMANIA MUSIC Administered by WB MUSIC CORP.
All Rights Reserved   Used by Permission

33

break through, there's no talk-ing to you.
do that, there's no turn-ing back.

It's so sad that you're leav - ing, take
I need time to move on. I need

time to be - lieve it, but af - ter all is
love to feel strong, 'cause I've had time to

said and done, you're going to be the lone - ly one, oh.
think it through, and may-be I'm too good for you, oh.

Bitch

Words and Music by
Meredith Brooks and Shelly Peiken

F#m

do what you do _____ and don't try to save _____

D

N.C.

A

me. I'm a bitch. I'm a lov-er, I'm a
bitch. I'm a tease. I'm a

E

Bsus2

child. I'm a moth-er. I'm a sin-ner. I'm a saint. I
god-dess on my knees. When you hurt, when you suf-fer, I'm your

D

A

do not feel a-shamed. I'm your hell. I'm your dream. I'm
an-gel un-der-cov-er. I've been numb. I'm re-vived. Can't

44

Black Hole Sun

Words and Music by
Chris Cornell

Won't you come? _____

Won't you come? _____

Won't you come? _____

Buddy Holly

Words and Music by
Rivers Cuomo

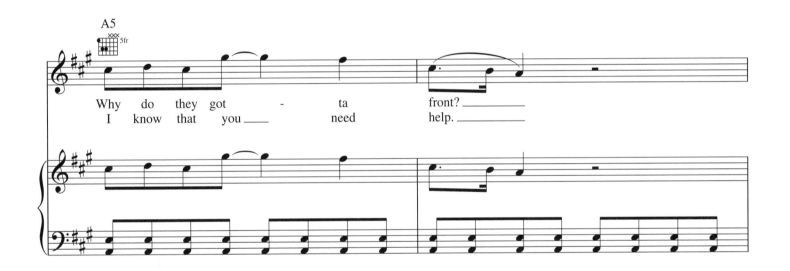

that made them so ___ vi - o - lent? ___
You need a guard - i - an. ___

(Woo hoo) But } you know ___ I'm yours, ___
(Woo hoo) And }

(Woo hoo) and I know ___ you're mine, ___ (Woo hoo and that's _

___ for all ___ time.) ___ Ooh wee ooh, I look just like Bud - dy Hol - ly.

Oh oh, and you're Mar - y Ty - ler Moore.

I don't care what they say a - bout us an - y - way.

I don't care 'bout that.

What's-a - mat - ter, what's a - mat - ter, what's-a - mat - ter you? What's a - mat - ter, babe, are you feel - in' blue?

Oh,   oh, _____ oh,   oh,   oh,   oh,   oh. _____

(And   that's _____ for   all _____   time.) _
                                                    (That's _

57

Creep

Words and Music by
Albert Hammond, Mike Hazlewood,
Thomas Yorke, Jonathan Greenwood,
Colin Greenwood, Edward O'Brien
and Philip Selway

Criminal

Words and Music by
Fiona Apple

Moderately

I've been a bad, __ bad __ girl; __ I've been care-less with a

del - i - cate __ man. __ And it's a sad, sad _____ world

when a girl will break a boy __ just be - cause __ she can. ____

Don't you tell me to __ de - ny _____ it; I've done wrong, __

__ and I wan-na suf-fer for __ my __ sins. I've come to you __'cause I __ need

guid - ance to be true, __ and I just don't know __ where I can __ be - gin. __

What I __ need __ is a good de - fense, __ 'cause I'm

feel - in' __ like __ a crim - i - nal. __ And I need to be re - deemed __ to the

one I've sinned a - gainst __ be - cause he's all I __ ev - er knew of love.

To Coda ⊕

CODA

Cm7

Eb   B   Ab   B

Let me know ___ the way ___ be - fore there's hell ___ to pay. ___

Eb   B   Ab7

Give me room ___ to lay ___ the law ___ and let ___ me go. ___

Eb   B   Ab   B

I've got to make ___ a play ___ to make my lov - er stay, ___

so what would an an - gel say, the dev - il wants to know. ___

___ What I need ___ is a

good de - fense, ___ 'cause I'm feel - in' ___ like ___ a crim - i - nal. ___

And I need to be ___ re - deemed ___ to the one ___

Damn, I Wish I Was Your Lover

Words and Music by
Sophie B. Hawkins

ev - er and ev - er and ev - er and ev - er. Give me an hour to kiss ___ you.

Walk through heav - en's door ___ I'm sure. ___ Don't need no doc - tor to feel ___ much bet - ter.

Let me in. ___ Ooh. (I wan-na live.) For -

ev - er and ev - er and ev - er and ev - er. ___

Fields of Gold

Music and Lyrics by
Sting

Flowing, moderately

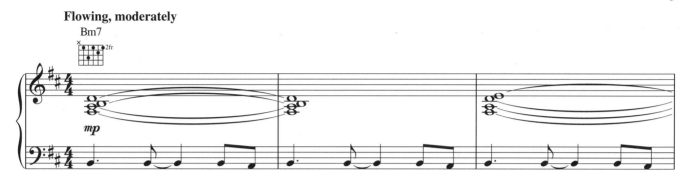

You'll re - mem - ber me,   when the west wind moves __ up a -
stay with me,   will you be my love __ a -

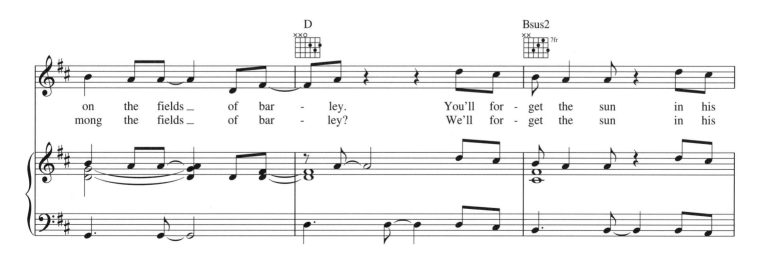

on the fields __ of bar - ley.   You'll for - get the sun in his
mong the fields __ of bar - ley?   We'll for - get the sun in his

From a Distance

Words and Music by
Julie Gold

Genie in a Bottle

Words and Music by
Steve Kipner, David Frank
and Pamela Sheyne

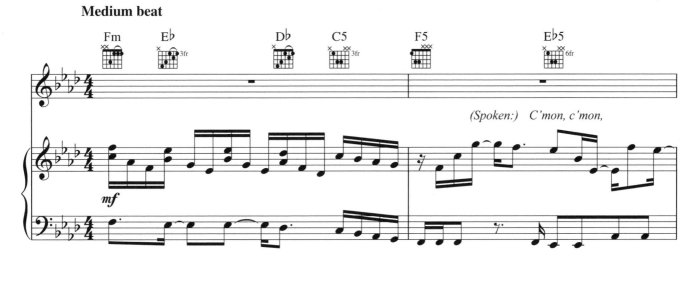

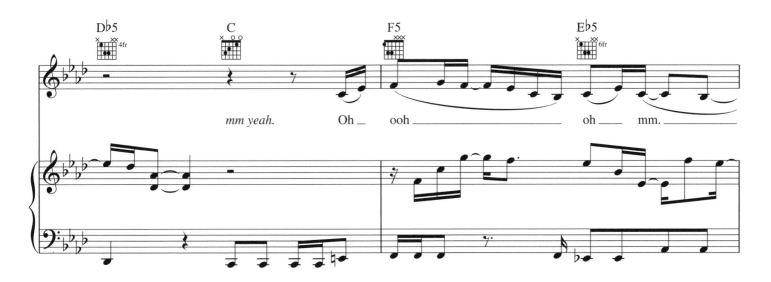

Good Riddance
(Time of Your Life)

Words by Billie Joe

Music by Green Day

some - thing un - pre - dict - a - ble, ___ but in the end ___ it's right. ___

___ I hope you had ___ the time ___ of ___ your life. ___

Have I Told You Lately

Words and Music by
Van Morrison

ease my trou-bles, that's __ what you do.

For the
Instrumental solo

morn - in' sun in all __ its glo - ry

greets the

day with hope and com - fort, too. __

You fill my life with laugh - ter

and some-how you make it bet - ter,

to the one.___ And have I told___ you late - ly that I love you? Have I told you there's no one else___ a - bove you? You fill my heart___ with glad - ness,___ take a - way___ my sad - ness, ease my trou - bles, that's___ what you

I Don't Want to Wait

Words and Music by
Paula Cole

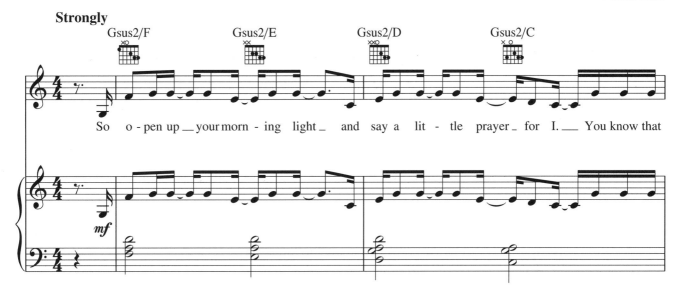

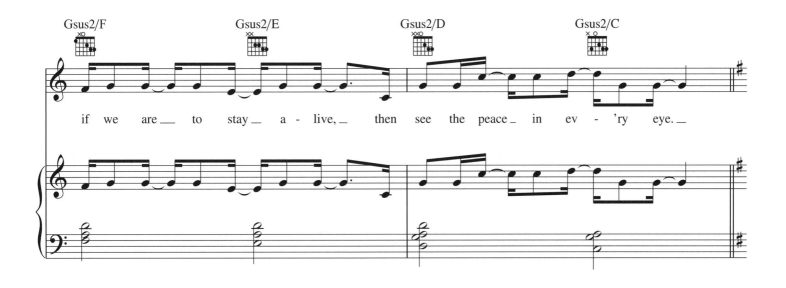

du du du __ du du du. __

She had two __ ba - bies,   one was six __ months, one __ was three,
He showed up __ all wet   on the rain - y front _____ step

in the war __ of for - ty - four. _____
wear-ing shrap - nel in his skin. _____

Ev - 'ry tel - e-phone ring,   ev - 'ry heart - beat sting - ing when she
And the war __ he saw   lives _ in - side _ him still. _ It's so

his fa-ther did. I want to be here now. ___ So o-pen up ___ your morn - ing light ___ and say a lit - tle prayer ___ for I. ___ You know that if we are ___ to stay ___ a - live, ___ then see the peace ___ in ev - 'ry eye. ___ I don't want to wait for our lives ___ to be o - ver. ___ I want ___

I Want It That Way

Words and Music by
Martin Sandberg and Andreas Carlsson

I Will Always Love You

featured in THE BODYGUARD

Words and Music by
Dolly Parton

will al - ways love you. _____ I will al - ways _____ love _

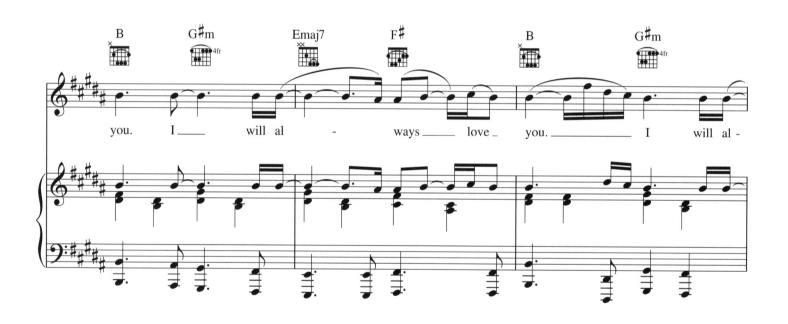

you. I _____ will al - ways _____ love you. _____ I will al -

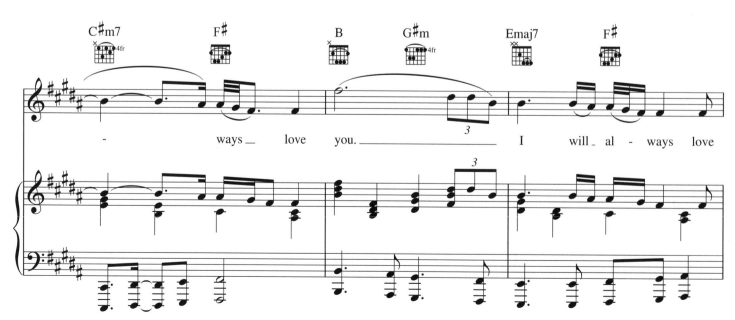

- ways _____ love you. _____ I will al - ways love

Additional Lyrics

3. I hope life treats you kind.
   And I hope you have all you've dreamed of.
   And I wish to you, joy and happiness.
   But above all this, I wish you love.

I'll Be

Words and Music by
Edwin McCain

* Recorded a half step lower.

Iris

from the Motion Picture CITY OF ANGELS

Words and Music by
John Rzeznik

And you can't

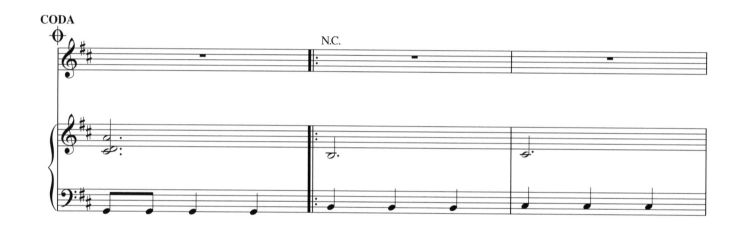

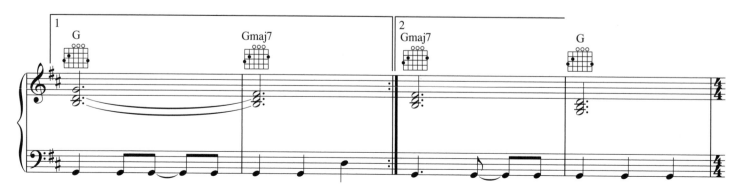

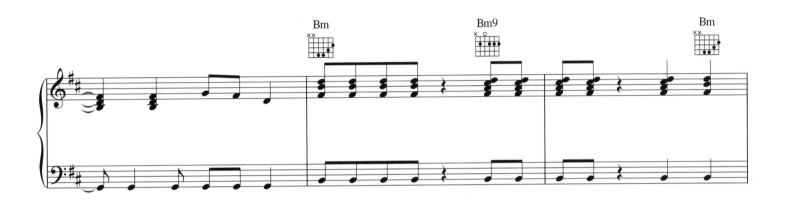

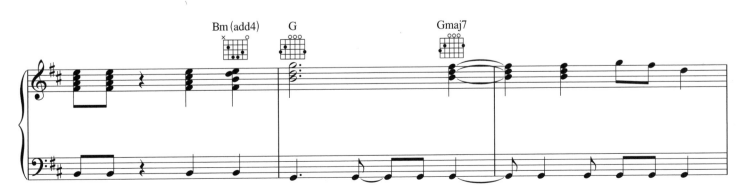

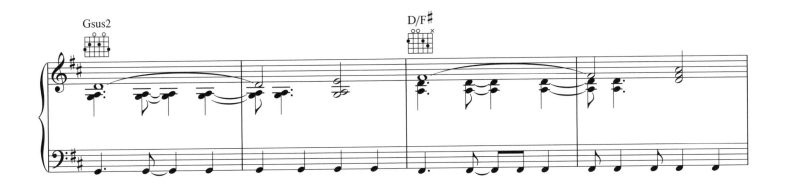

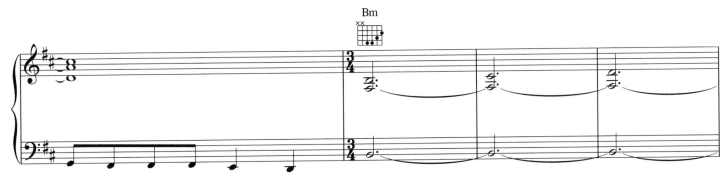

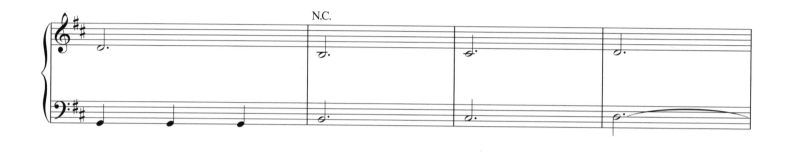

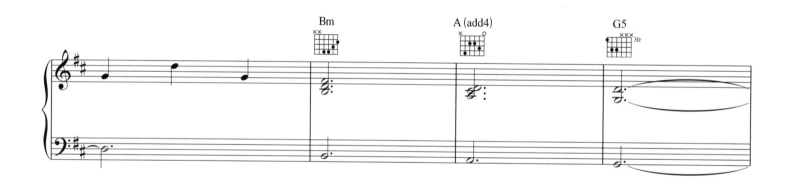

And I ____ don't want the world ____ to see ____ me

Jeremy

Lyric by Eddie Vedder

Music by Jeff Ament

Alternative Rock

Linger

Lyrics by Dolores O'Riordan

Music by
Dolores O'Riordan and Noel Hogan

150

Do you have to let it lin - ger? Do you have to, do you have to, do you have to let it lin - ger? _____

To Coda ✛

Oh, I thought the world of you. _____ I thought

Instrumental solo

noth - ing could _____ go wrong, _____ but I was wrong. _____

Livin' la Vida Loca

Words and Music by
Desmond Child and Robi Rosa

She's in - to new sen - sa - tions,
Woke up in New York Cit - y

new kicks in the can - dle - light. __
in a funk - y cheap ho - tel. __
She's got a
She took my heart and she

new ad - dic - tion
took my mon - ey.
for ev - 'ry day and night. __ She'll
She must -'ve slipped me a sleep - in' pill. __ She

F#m

(1., 3.) make you take __ your clothes __ off and __ go danc - ing in __ the rain. __
(2.) nev - er drinks __ the wa - ter and makes __ you or - der French __ cham - pagne. __

G#m

She's liv-in' la vi-da lo-ca.

-ca.

160

Losing My Religion

Words and Music by
William Berry, Peter Buck,
Michael Mills and Michael Stipe

164

Man in the Box

Written by
Jerry Cantrell, Layne Staley,
Sean Kinney and Michael Starr

Moderate Rock

Da da da da da da da da da da.

I'm the man in the box.
I'm the dog who gets beat.
Guitar solo ad lib.

Bur - ied in
Shove my nose

my eyes. (Now you've sewn them shut.)

you've sewn them shut.) Da da da da da da

da da da. Da da da

da da da da da da.

Mr. Jones

Words by Adam Duritz

Music by
Adam Duritz and David Bryson

ti - ful.   Man, I wish I was beau - ti - ful.   So, come

dance this si - lence down ____ through the morn - ing.

Sha - la - la - la - la - la - la - la, ____ yeah.

Uh huh,   yeah. ____

y wants to pass____ as cats. We all want to be big,____

____ big stars,__ yeah, but we got dif-f'rent rea - sons for that.

Be - lieve__ in me be-cause I don't be - lieve__ in an -

y - thing and I_____ want to be some - one to____ be - lieve,

178

to be - lieve, to ___ be - lieve, yeah. ___

G   C   F   G

Mis - ter Jones and ___ me stum - bling through the bar -
Mis - ter Jones and ___ me star - ing at the vid -

C   F

ri - o. Yeah, we stare at the beau - ti - ful wom - en. "She's per -
e - o. When I look at the tel - e - vi - sion, I want to

G   C

fect for you. Man, there's got to be ___ some - bod - y for me." ___ I want to be Bob Dyl -
see me star - ing ___ right back at me. ___ We all want to be big

MMM Bop

Words and Music by
Isaac Hanson, Taylor Hanson
and Zac Hanson

184

My Heart Will Go On
(Love Theme from 'Titanic')
from the Paramount and Twentieth Century Fox Motion Picture TITANIC

Lyric by Will Jennings

Music by James Horner

189

Once   more   you o - pen the door

and you're here   in my heart, and   my heart will   go

To Coda ⊕

on   and   on.

Love   can touch us   one time   and   last for   a

ev - er this way. ___ You are safe in my

heart, and my heart will go on and on. ___

ff decrescendo to end

Mm. ___

One of Us

Words and Music by
Eric Bazilian

Slowly, moving

slob like one of us, just a stran - ger on the bus_

_ trying to make his way _ home, _ just trying to make his way _

_ home, _ just like a ho - ly roll - ing _ stone? _

Only Wanna Be with You

Words and Music by
Darius Carlos Rucker, Everett Dean Felber,
Mark William Bryan and James George Sonefeld

You look at me, _____ you got
Put on a lit - tle Dyl - an,
Some - times I won - der

noth - ing left ___ to say. ___
sit - ting on ___ a fence. ___
if it will ev - er end. ___

I moan and pout ___ at you ___ un - til
I say, "That line ___ is great." ___ You ask
You get so mad ___ at me when I go ___

___ I get ___ my ___ way.
___ me what ___ I meant by
___ out with ___ my ___ friends.

I won't dance, ___
"Said I shot a man ___ named Gray, ___
Some - times you're cra - zy

202

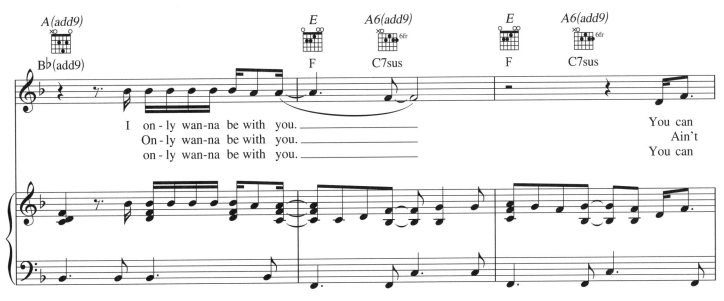

204

on - ly wan - na be with you. ____

on - ly wan - na be with you, _____

on - ly wan - na be with you, _____

on - ly wan-na be with you. _____

Peaches

Words and Music by
Chris Ballew, Dave Dederer
and Jason Finn

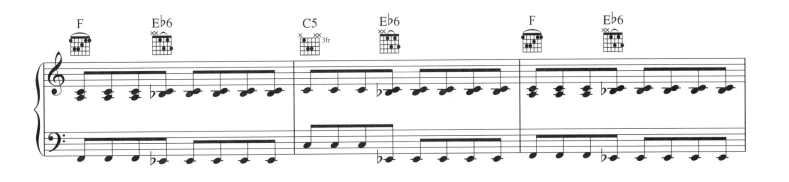

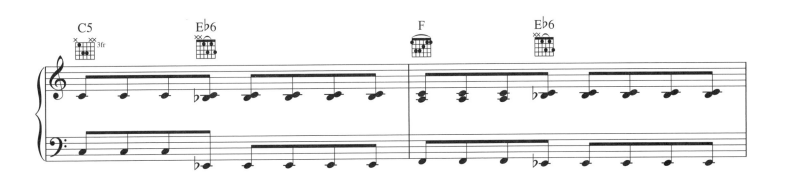

Mil - lions of peach - es,   peach - es for me.

Mil - lions of peach - es,   peach - es for free.

Mil - lions of peach - es, peach - es for me.

Mil - lions of peach - es, peach - es for free. Look out!

D.S. al Coda

Semi-Charmed Life

Words and Music by
Stephan Jenkins

And I speak to you __ like the cho-rus to the verse. Chop an-oth-er line like a co-da with a curse. Come on like a freak show takes the stage. We give them the games we play. __ She say, "I want some-thing __ else to get me through this sem-i-charmed kind of life, __ ba - by, ba - by. I want some - thing else, __

The beach gives a feel-ing, an earth-y feel-ing. I be-lieve in the faith that grows, and the four right chords can make me cry. When I'm with you I feel like I could die, and that would be all right, all right. And when the plane came in, she said she was crash-ing.

218

bye, _____ good - bye. _____

Doo doo doot doo doo doot _ doo. Doo doo doot doo doo doot _ doo.

Doo doo doot doo doo doot _ doo. The sky was gold, _

Sex and Candy

Words and Music by
John Wozniak

Mellow Rock

Hang - ing 'round _ down-town by my - self _ and I _ had
Hang - ing 'round _ down-town by my - self _ and I've _ had

so much _ time _ to sit and think a - bout _ my - self. _ 'N' then there she was
too much _ caf - feine and I was think-ing 'bout _ my - self. _ 'N' then there she was _

like dou - ble cher - ry pie, _ yeah, there she was _
in plat - form dou - ble suede, _ yeah, there she was _

Recorded a half step lower.

224

Shine

Words and Music by
Ed Roland

Moderate Rock

(1.,3.) Give me a word, give __ me a sign, show me where to look, tell __ me what will I

(2.) Love is in the wa-ter, love __ is in the air, show me where to look, tell __ me will love be

find, __ what will I _____ find? _____

there, __ will love be _____ there? _____

* Recorded a half step higher.

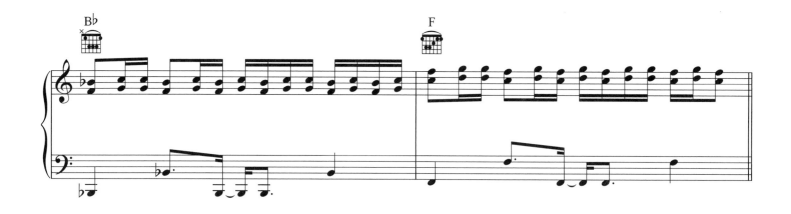

Double-time feel

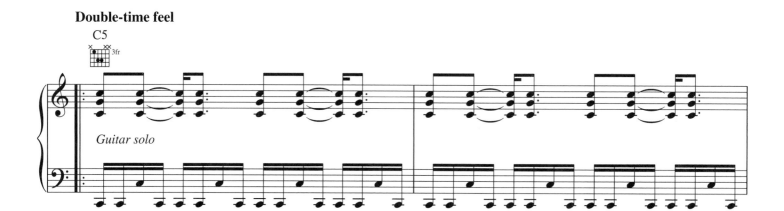

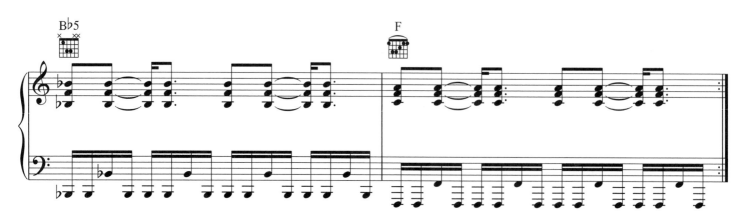

End Double-time feel

D.S. al Coda

Double-time feel

CODA

light shine _ down.   I'm gon-na   let   it   shine, _ I'm gon-na let it   shine, _

heav-en's lit-tle light gon-na shine on   me. __ I said   hey,   yeah, _   hey,   yeah, _

heav-en's lit - tle light shine on me. (Shine,)_____ shine on me,__

_____ yeah._____ (Shine,)_____ come on and

End Double-time feel

shine.

232

Smells Like Teen Spirit

Words and Music by
Kurt Cobain, Krist Novoselic
and Dave Grohl

Load up ___ on guns, ___ bring ___ your friends.
I'm worse ___ at what ___ I ___ do best,
And I ___ for-get ___ just why ___ I ___ taste. ___

It's fun ___ to lose ___ and to ___ pre-tend. ___ She's o-ver-bored,
and for ___ this gift ___ I feel ___ blessed. ___ Our lit-tle trap ___
Oh, yeah, ___ I guess ___ it makes ___ me smile. ___ I found ___ it hard;

234

Stay

Words and Music by
Lisa Loeb

Guitar: to match recording, capo I.

And you said _ that I was na - ive and _ I thought _ that I was strong.

I thought, _ "Hey, I can leave, I can leave, oh." But now I know _ that I ___ was wrong 'cause I

missed you, yeah, _____ missed you.

You said you caught me 'cause you want me and one day you'll let me go. You try to

Tearin' Up My Heart

Words and Music by
Max Martin and Kristian Lundin

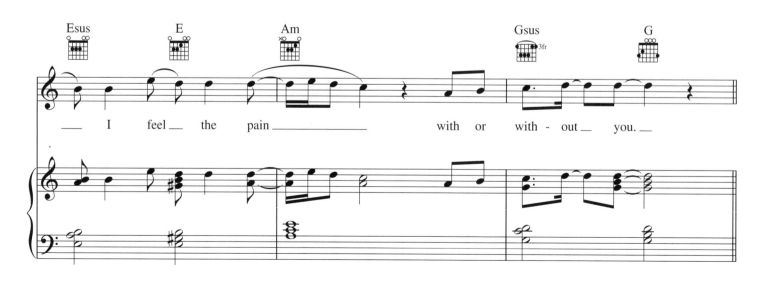

3 AM

Lyrics by Rob Thomas

Music by
Rob Thomas, Brian Yale,
John Leslie Goff and John Joseph Stanley

some - times, and the rain's gon - na wash a - way; _ I be - lieve it. rain's gon - na wash a - way; _ I be - lieve

this.

D.S. al Coda

CODA

out - side   it's stopped

rain - ing, _____ yeah. But she _ says, "Ba - by, _____

Two Princes

Words and Music by
Spin Doctors

One has   dia-monds   in __ his pock - ets   (that's some bread, _ now.)
Mar-ry   him,   your fath - er   will _ con - done _ you.   (How 'bout   that, __ now.) You

This   one,   he wants   to   buy _ you   rock - ets,   (ain't   in   his   head, _ now.)
mar-ry   me,   your   fa - ther   will _ dis - own __ you.   (He'll   eat   his   hat, __ now.)

Yeah, _____ yeah,   yeah. _____   (Di   di   ga

dip.   Di   dip   dip   di   dip.   Ba   dee - dle - ee   di ba du ba du ba du ba   du ba du ba du ba du ba.)

-ets (and that's some bread,_ now.) This one, he wants to buy_ you rock

-ets, (ain't in his head,_ now.) Mar-ry him or mar-ry me. I'm_

_ the one that loves you, ba-by. Can't you see?_ I ain't got no fu-ture or a fam-'ly tree,_ but

Solo ends Said

Under the Bridge

Words and Music by
Anthony Kiedis, Flea,
John Frusciante and Chad Smith

262

Virtual Insanity

Words and Music by
Jason Kay and Toby Smith

* Recorded a half step lower.

Dm   A+

Ooh, oh, this vir - tu - al___ in - san - i - ty___ we're liv -

B♭maj7   Gm7   Am7

ing in,   it's got___ to change, ___ yeah. ___ Things ___

Dm   A+

___ will nev - er be the same   and I can't__ go on

B♭maj7   Gm7   Am7

while we're liv - ing in,   oh,   oh, vir - tu - al in - san - i -

275

Vision of Love

Words and Music by
Mariah Carey and Ben Margulies

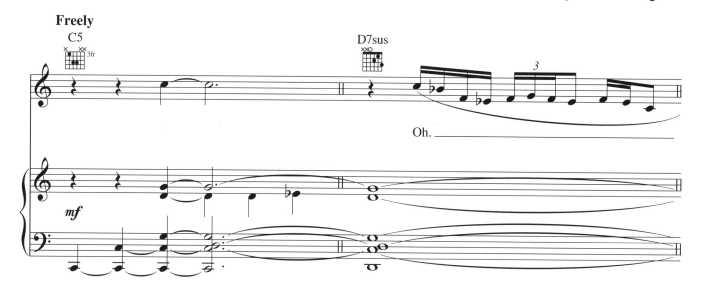

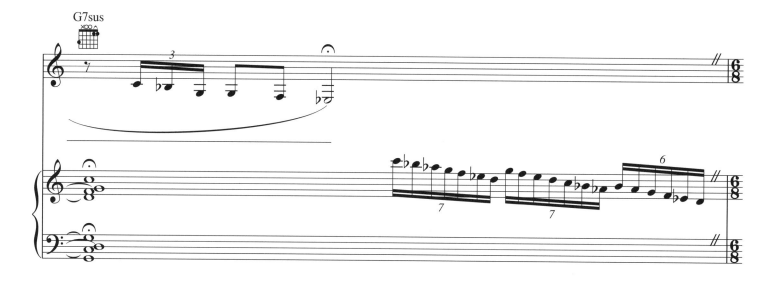

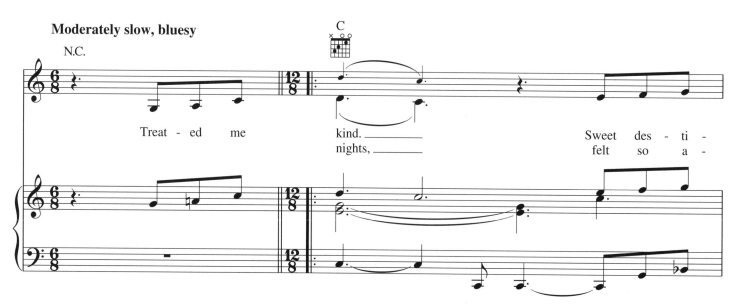

me. ____ I had a vi - sion of love, ____ and it was all _____

that you

A tempo

turned out ___ to be. _____

Oh ____ oh. _____

rit.

Wannabe

Words and Music by
Geri Halliwell, Emma Bunton,
Melanie Brown, Melanie Chisholm,
Victoria Adams and Matthew Rowebottom

Waterfalls

Words and Music by
Marqueze Etheridge, Lisa Nicole Lopes,
Rico R. Wade, Pat Brown
and Ramon Murray

Rap ends

Don't go chas - ing wa - ter - falls. Please stick to the

riv - ers and the lakes that you're used ___ to. I know that you're

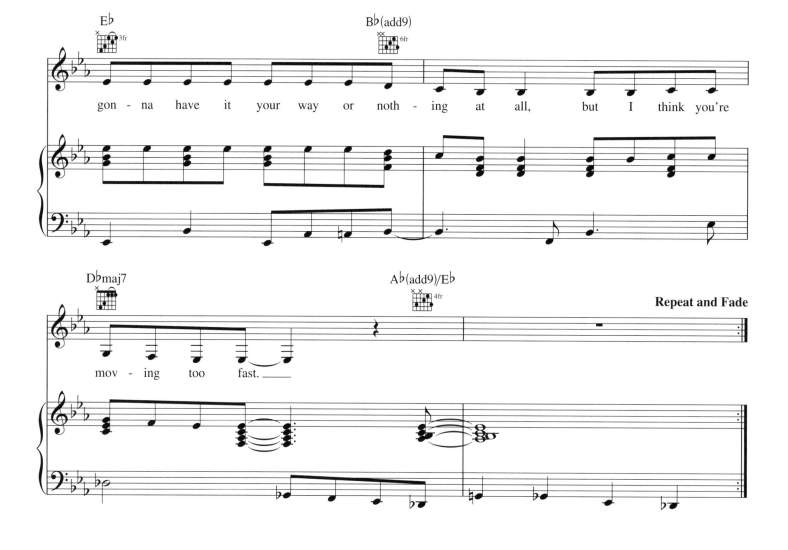

Additional Lyrics

Rap: I seen a rainbow yesterday
But too many storms have come and gone
Leavin' a trace of not one God-given ray
Is it because my life is ten shades of gray
I pray all ten fade away
Seldom praise Him for the sunny days
And like His promise is true
Only my faith can undo
The many chances I blew
To bring life to anew
Clear blue and unconditional skies
Have dried the tears from my eyes
No more lonely cries
My only bleedin' hope
Is for the folk who can't cope
Wit such an endurin' pain
That it keeps 'em in the pourin' rain
Who's to blame
For tootin' caine in your own vein
What a shame
You shoot and aim for someone else's brain
You claim the insane
And name this day in time
For fallin' prey to crime
I say the system got you victim to your own mind
Dreams are hopeless aspirations
In hopes of comin' true
Believe in yourself
The rest is up to me and you

Who Will Save Your Soul

Lyrics and Music by
Jewel Kilcher

Originally sung an octave lower.

Wonderwall

Words and Music by
Noel Gallagher

And all ___ the roads ___ we have ___ to walk ___ are wind-
And all ___ the roads ___ that lead ___ you there ___ were wind-

- ing, ___ and all ___ the lights ___ that lead ___ us there ___ are blind - ing. }
- ing, ___ and all ___ the lights ___ that light ___ the way ___ are blind - ing. }

There are man - y things ___ that I ___ would like ___ to say ___ to you ___ but I don't know how. ___

{ Be-cause }
{ I said } may - be ___

you're gon - na be the one that saves me, _____ and af - ter all, _____

you're my won - der - wall. _____

I said may - be _____

you're gon - na be the one that saves me, _____ and af - ter all, _____

You Get What You Give

Words and Music by
Gregg Alexander and Rick Nowels

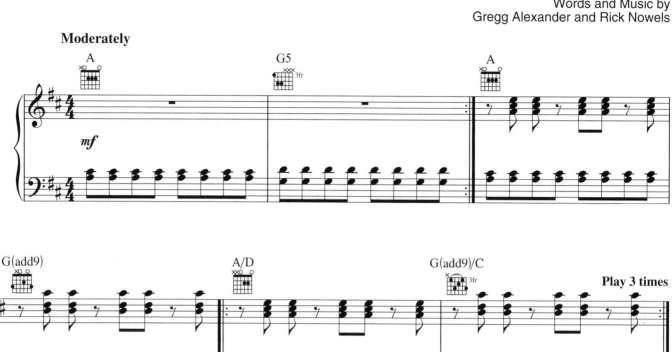

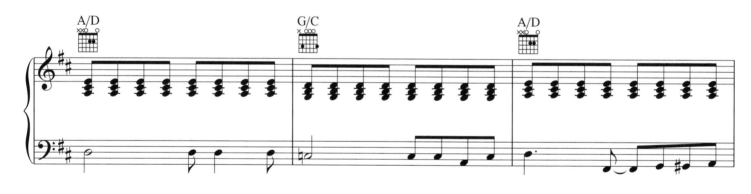

Wake up, kids. __ We've got the dream-er's dis - ease. __
Frien - e - mies, __ who when you're down ain't your friend. __
Four a. m., __ we ran a mir - a - cle mile. __

light. If you feel your dreams are dy - in', ___ hold tight. ___
friend. You feel your tree is break - in' ___ just then. ___

You've got the mu - sic in you. ___ Don't let go. You've got the mu - sic in you. _

___ One dance left. This world is gon - na pull through. _ Don't give up.

You got a rea - son to live. ___ Can't for - get. We on - ly get what we give. _

could fall a - part. ___ You'll be O - K, ___ fol - low your heart. ___

You're in harm's way. ___ I'm right be - hind. ___ Now, say you're mine. ___

You've got the mu - sic in you. ___ Don't let go. You've got the mu - sic in you. ___

Health in - sur - ance rip - off, ly - ing
Fash - ion shoots with Beck and Han - son,

F. D. A., big bank - ers buy - ing. Fake com - put - er crash - es din - ing, clon - ing while they're mul - ti - ply - ing.
Court - ney Love and Mar - 'lyn Man - son. You're all fakes, run to your man - sions.

Come a - round, we'll kick your ass in. Don't let go.
Don't give up.

Repeat and Fade | **Optional Ending**

One dance left.
Can't for - get.

You Oughta Know

Lyrics by Alanis Morissette

Music by
Alanis Morissette and Glen Ballard

You're Still the One

Words and Music by
Shania Twain and R.J. Lange